Ancient
EGYPT

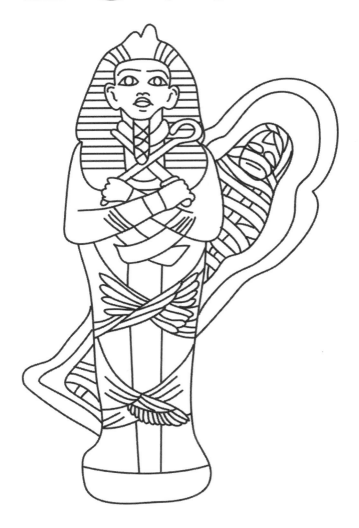

Table of Contents

Where in the world is EGYPT?

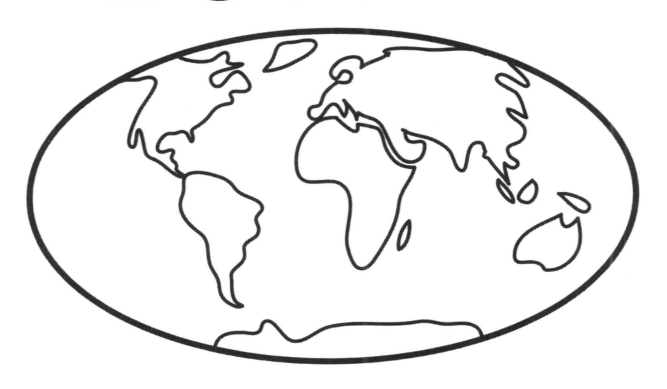

EGYPT ON THE MAP

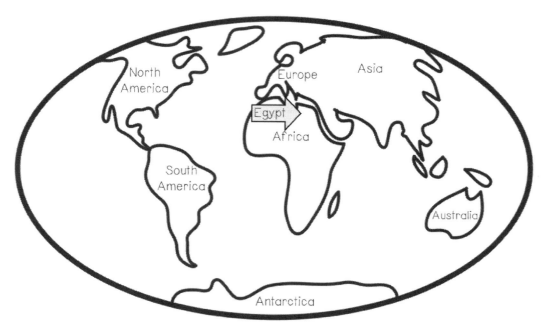

Here is a picture of our globe. We have 7 continents: North America, South America, Europe, Asia, Africa, Australia and Antarctica. Egypt is a country located in the North part of Africa. People enjoy learning about Egypt because it's a country that has been around for thousands of years and has a fascinating culture and history.

Egypt has a hot, dry desert climate with little rain. Cairo is the capital of Egypt. Ancient Egyptians depended on the Nile River to survive. They used this water for drinking, washing, as well as watering crops and animals. The Nile is the longest river in the world. It starts south of Egypt and flows from south to north where it ends in the Mediterranean Sea. In the north where the Nile empties into the sea is the Nile River Delta. This land is perfect for growing crops and this area of Egypt is covered in farms!

EGYPT ON THE MAP

Read the passage. Use the passage to answer the questions. Use the correct color crayon to show where you found your answer in the text.

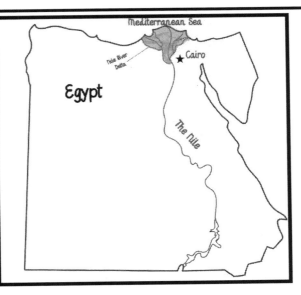

Egypt is a country located in Africa. Egypt has a hot, dry desert climate with little rain. Egypt is home to the longest river in the world, the Nile River. Ancient Egyptians depended on the Nile River to survive. They used this water for drinking, washing, as well as watering crops and animals. In the north where the Nile empties into the Mediterranean Sea is the Nile River Delta.

This land is perfect for growing crops, so this area of Egypt is covered in farms! Along the Nile are many cities. Cairo is the capital and largest city in Egypt. Near Cairo you can see many cool and ancient monuments like the pyramids!

1. What is Egypt's climate like?

_____

_____

2. What did ancient Egyptians use the Nile for?

_____

_____

EGYPT ON THE MAP

Use the word back below to label the map correctly.

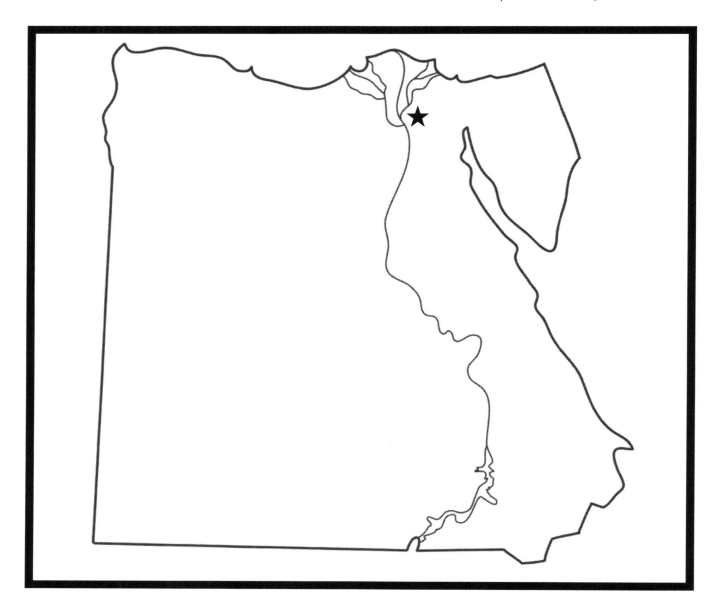

Egypt   The
               Nile

          Nile River
            Delta
                              Cairo

EGYPT ON THE MAP

Follow the directions to correctly label and color the map.

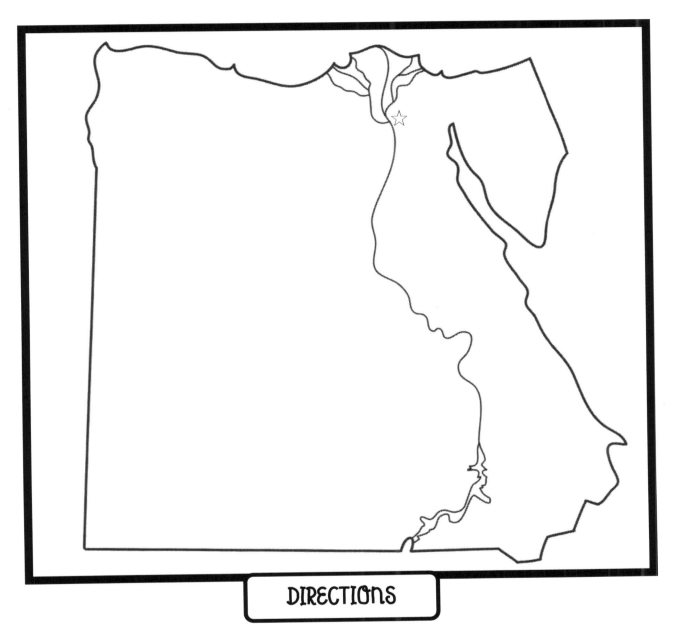

DIRECTIONS

1. Label the Nile River. Trace it BLUE.

2. Label the Nile River Delta. Color it GREEN.

3. Label Cairo. Color the star RED.

4. Label Egypt. Color all of Egypt YELLOW.

EGYPT ON THE MAP

Search and find the words hidden in the word search!

E	N	W	P	I	O	R	I	A	C
L	I	V	S	N	F	A	L	K	J
A	L	B	D	R	G	H	P	A	M
S	E	A	F	T	I	G	E	T	O
P	R	F	D	E	L	T	A	P	I
N	I	R	E	A	H	T	C	Y	R
E	V	I	S	H	M	I	Z	G	E
D	E	C	E	I	S	D	W	E	W
I	R	A	R	L	P	E	A	N	L
P	O	G	T	E	S	M	R	A	F

Egypt	Desert	Delta
Cairo	Farms	Africa
Nile River	Sea	Map

EGYPT ON THE MAP

After completing the "Egypt on the Map" activities, take this quiz
by **drawing a line** to the correct answer.

.   What continent is Egypt
    located on?

                                                a. The Nile River

2.   What is the capital of
     Egypt?

                                                  b. Africa

3.   What is the name of the
     longest river in the world
     that flows through Egypt?

                                         c. Nile River Delta

4.   Where can you find many
     farms in Egypt?

                                                 d. Cairo

Who were the ANCIENT EGYPTIANS?

WHO WERE THE ANCIENT EGYPTIANS?

Rulers called
Pharaohs

Ancient history is the study of events from the beginning of human history. Ancient Egypt was one of the first civilizations. The ancient Egyptian's empire grew along the Nile River in Egypt 5,000 years ago. Their empire reigned for almost 3,000 years! The Egyptians are so interesting because they did many unique, amazing and mysterious things during their empire. Some of the coolest things the Egyptians are known for are building the pyramids, mummifying their dead, being ruled by Pharaohs and writing in an ancient form of picture writing called hieroglyphics!

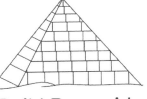
Build Pyramids

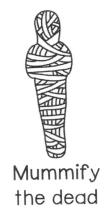
Mummify
the dead

Write with
hieroglyphics

WHO WERE THE ANCIENT EGYPTIANS?

Read the passage. Use the passage to answer the questions. Use the correct color crayon to show where you found your answer in the text.

 The ancient Egyptians formed one of the first civilizations. Their empire grew along the Nile River in Egypt 5,000 years ago. It lasted for almost 3,000 years! The Egyptians are known for doing many amazing things during their empire such as being ruled by Pharaohs, creating a type of picture writing called hieroglyphics, mummifying their dead and building amazing structures like the pyramids!

1. How long did the Ancient Egyptian's empire last?

_____

_____

2. What are two things the Ancient Egyptians did during their empire?

_____

_____

WHO WERE THE ANCIENT EGYPTIANS?

Color each picture and trace the word

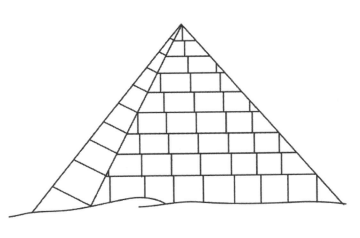

Pyramid

Pharaoh

Mummy Hieroglyphics

WHO WERE THE ANCIENT EGYPTIANS?

Draw a line from the Ancient Egyptian to each of the things he would have done or had in ancient Egypt.

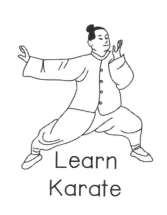

Learn Karate

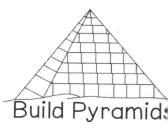

Build Pyramids

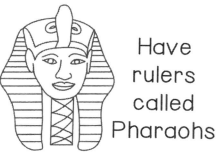

Have rulers called Pharaohs

Wear Togas

Write with hieroglyphics

Mummify the dead

WHO WERE THE ANCIENT EGYPTIANS?

Color the Egyptians!

WHO WERE THE ANCIENT EGYPTIANS?

Search and find the words hidden in the word search!

F	E	P	Y	R	A	M	I	D	R
R	M	H	A	O	M	E	A	P	A
U	U	E	M	U	M	M	Y	H	N
L	U	L	K	A	H	P	I	A	C
E	Y	U	I	N	E	I	C	R	I
R	P	R	P	F	I	R	T	A	E
E	H	S	H	U	R	E	N	O	N
M	W	R	I	T	I	N	G	H	T
P	O	A	O	L	Y	A	Y	P	N
I	H	I	S	T	O	R	Y	R	U

Mummy   Pyramid   Empire

Ancient   Ruler   History

Writing   Pharaoh

WHO WERE THE ANCIENT EGYPTIANS?

Write at least 3 new things you learned about ancient Egypt in the lines below. Use complete sentences. Draw a picture to match in the box.

WHO WERE THE ANCIENT EGYPTIANS?

After completing the "Who were the Egyptians" activities, take this quiz by **drawing a line** to the correct answer.

1. Why do we call Egypt's history Ancient?

    a. 5,000 years

2. How many years did the Egyptian's empire last?

    b. Building pyramids and writing in hieroglyphics

3. What are 2 things the Ancient Egyptians are known for?

    c. It took place thousands of years ago.

4. How many years ago did the Ancient Egyptians establish their empire?

    d. 3,000 years

What did the ancient Egyptians **EAT?**

ANCIENT EGYPTIAN FOOD

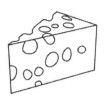   

The Egyptians had plenty of fresh food to keep them healthy thanks to the Nile River. They enjoyed three meals a day. The Egyptians ate with their fingers and carefully washed their hands with water before and after every meal. At everyday meals, Egyptians squatted over their food on a large mat. The Egyptians got most of their food from the Nile. They caught birds and collected eggs from the nests along the shore and caught fish in nets or on hooked lines. Bread was a staple of the Egyptian diet. It was eaten at every meal! Breads were sometimes sweetened with honey. They ate vegetables such as lentils, radishes, onions, garlic and green peas. Some fruits they enjoyed were figs, dates and grapes. Beer was the main drink of the Ancient Egyptians. It was made from grains. Children drank the milk from cows, sheep, goats and donkeys. They also made cheese and butter. The upper-class commonly dined on meat, fruit, vegetables, and honey-sweetened cakes or bread with wines made from grapes. The lower-class ate a diet of bread, fish, beans, onions and garlic washed down with a beer made from grains.

ANCIENT EGYPTIAN FOOD

Read the passage. Use the passage to answer the questions. Use the correct color crayon to show where you found your answer in the text.

The Egyptians had plenty of fresh food to keep them healthy. They ate three meals a day with their fingers. Much of their food was found in the Nile! They caught birds, gathered eggs from nests on the shore and caught fish to eat. Bread was a staple of the Egyptian diet. Breads were sometimes sweetened with honey. Beer was their main drink. They ate vegetables such as garlic, radishes, onions, and green peas. Some fruits they enjoyed were figs, dates and grapes.

1. What foods did the Egyptians find in the Nile?

_____

_____

2. What are two fruits the Egyptians enjoyed?

_____

_____

ANCIENT EGYPTIAN FOOD

Color the pictures that show food the ancient Egyptians ate yellow. Color the foods that they did not eat red.

ANCIENT EGYPTIAN FOOD

Sketch a drawing of an Ancient Egyptian Meal. Add labels to your drawing. Use the lines below to explain your drawings.

ANCIENT EGYPTIAN FOOD

Use what you've learned to compare and contrast the foods the ancient Egyptians ate and the food you eat in the pyramids below!

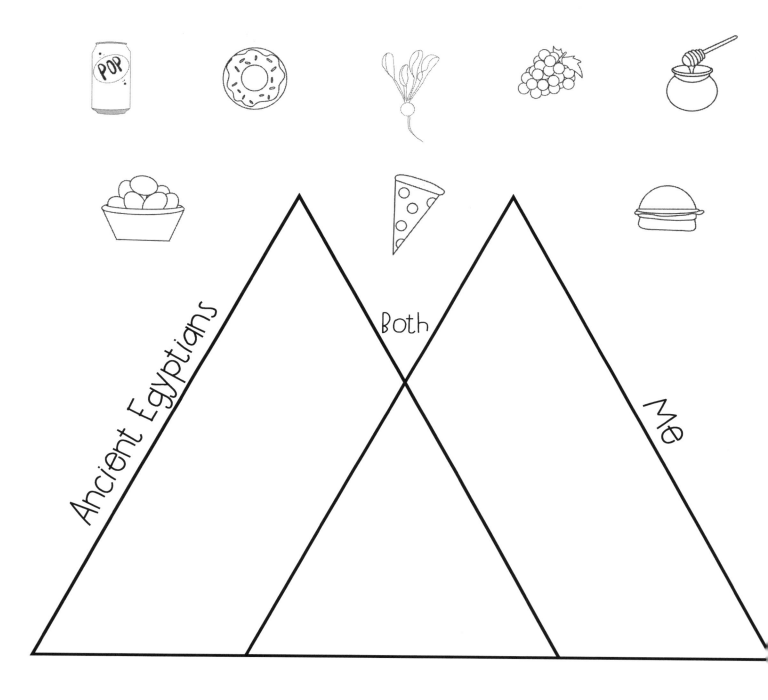

ANCIENT EGYPTIAN FOOD

With the help of a grownup, taste one or more of the foods that the Ancient Egyptians would have eaten. Fill in the information below.

Color the foods you want to try:

Food Tasting

What food(s) did you try?	Did you like it?

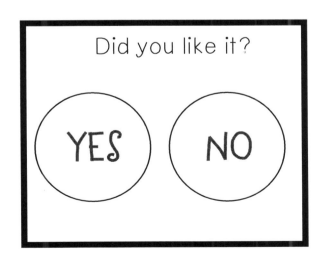

YES   NO

ANCIENT EGYPTIAN FOOD

Search and find the words hidden in the word search!

H	O	H	R	A	D	F	I	P	S
R	Y	O	S	G	I	F	B	O	C
A	E	N	B	R	E	A	R	C	H
D	O	N	I	O	N	C	E	H	E
I	N	N	O	F	P	I	A	E	E
S	R	A	D	I	S	H	D	O	S
E	H	V	B	S	N	O	E	P	E
M	I	L	K	H	M	N	L	A	L
A	R	W	D	X	O	E	R	S	A
S	G	G	E	L	M	Y	T	I	Y

Bread   Eggs   Honey

Milk   Fish   Figs

Radish   Onion   Cheese

ANCIENT EGYPTIAN FOOD

Write about what you would eat in a day if you lived in ancient Egypt. Use complete sentences. Draw a picture to match in the box.

ANCIENT EGYPTIAN FOOD

After completing the "Ancient Egyptian Food" activities, take this quiz by **drawing a line** to the correct answer.

1. What is a food Egyptians ate at every meal?

   a. Figs, dates and grapes

2. What did Egyptian children drink?

   b. Bread

3. What fruits did the Ancient Egyptians eat?

   c. The Nile

4. Where did the Egyptians get most of their food?

   d. Milk from cows, sheep, goats and donkey

How did the Egyptians **LIVE?**

Clothes and Makeup

Egyptian Man

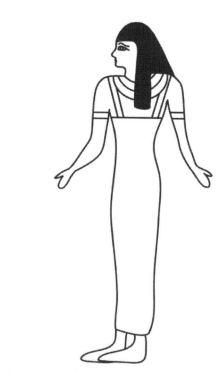

Egyptian Woman

The ancient Egyptians dressed very different than we do today! Men wore skirts that wrapped around their waist and hung above the knee. Both men and women used eye makeup. It was called kohl and was a black, crushed mineral. Women wore dresses that were plain white or beige. The dresses were long from shoulder to ankle. Women kept their hair and nails colored using henna. If they kept their hair long, they took good care of it and brushed it with an ivory comb. The Ancient Egyptians loved to wear jewelry. Both men and women wore jewelry like collars, gold and bronze arm bands and bracelets. Women also sometimes wore headbands.

Home, Work and School

scribe

house made of
mud bricks

farmer

Whether they were rich or poor, the ancient Egyptians houses were made of mud bricks. It could be one to three stories tall. The house size depended on the father's job! There was much work to be done in ancient Egypt. Many Egyptian men were builders, hunters, farmers, craftsmen, store owners and scribes. Women were in charge of running their household. Only the smartest and wealthiest children went to school. There they learned to be scribes. Scribes were important because they were usually the only ones who could read and write. Students memorized the hieroglyphic signs and practiced writing.

EGYPTIAN DAILY LIFE

Read the passage. Use the passage to answer the questions. Use the correct color crayon to show where you found your answer in the text.

The Egyptians lived in houses made of mud bricks. Many Egyptian men were builders, hunters, farmers, craftsmen, store owners and scribes. Women were in charge of running their household. The smartest and wealthiest children got to go to school and learned to be scribes. Scribes were important because they were the only ones who could read and write. The Ancient Egyptians loved to wear jewelry. Both men and women wore jewelry like collars, and gold and bronze arm bands. Both men and women also used eye makeup. Women wore dresses that were plain white or beige. The dresses were long from shoulder to ankle. Men wore skirts that wrapped around their waist and hung above the knee. Kids didn't have to wear clothes until they became teenagers!

1. What is something that both men and women wore?

_____

_____

2. List two jobs Egyptian men could've had.

_____

_____

EGYPTIAN DAILY LIFE

Color the Egyptians doing their jobs.

farmer

scribe

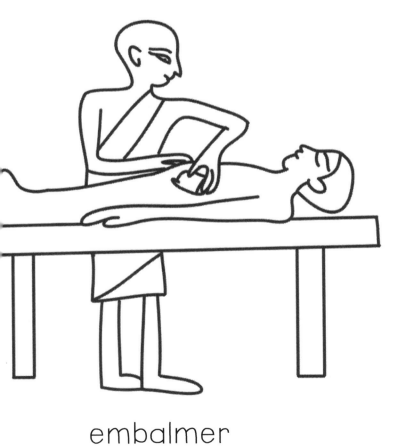

embalmer

hunter

EGYPTIAN DAILY LIFE

Sketch a drawing of an Ancient Egyptian! Give this Egyptian clothes, jewelry, makeup and accessories. Label your drawing.

EGYPTIAN DAILY LIFE

Color the pyramids that have the name of a job the ancient Egyptians could have had.

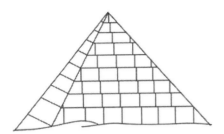

farmer

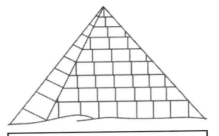

dog walker

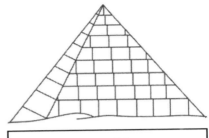

scribe

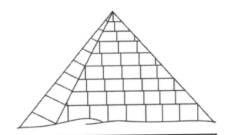

teacher

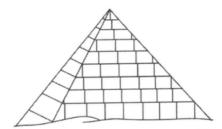

Police officer

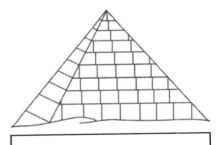

store owner

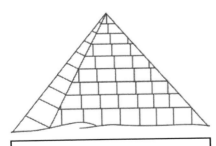

builder

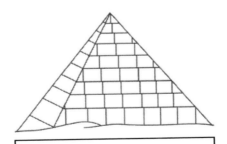

craftsman

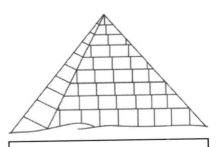

hunter

Egyptian neck collar. Color, cut & Tie with yarn.

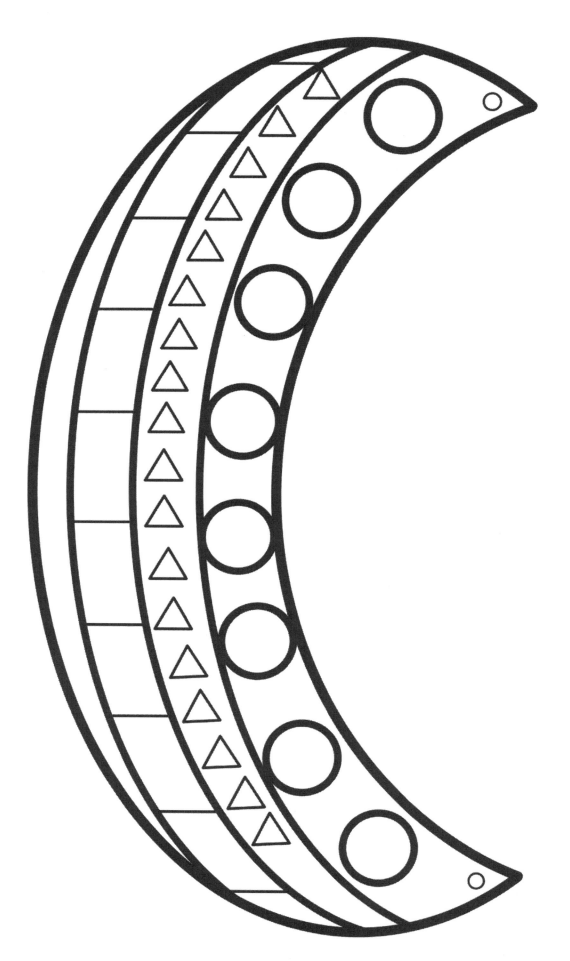

EGYPTIAN DAILY LIFE

Search and find the words hidden in the word search!

A	C	A	D	S	T	F	Y	S	H
K	O	H	L	E	L	A	C	S	U
S	L	E	R	O	Q	R	U	D	N
P	L	S	L	H	I	M	I	A	T
O	A	K	T	B	W	E	O	C	E
L	R	I	E	N	E	R	P	V	R
K	C	R	D	E	R	J	L	B	P
T	T	T	H	H	O	U	S	E	O
J	E	W	E	L	R	Y	K	N	S
W	P	M	N	R	T	H	G	M	L

Jewelry   Mud   Collar

Farmer   Scribe   Hunter

Skirt   House   Kohl

EGYPTIAN DAILY LIFE

Write about what job you would have if you lived in ancient Egypt. Use complete sentences. Draw a picture to match in the box.

EGYPTIAN DAILY LIFE

After completing the "Egyptian Daily Life" activities, take this quiz by **drawing a line** to the correct answer.

What are some jobs an
Egyptian man could've had?

a. Jewelry and
makeup

What job would an Egyptian
woman have had?

b. Run their
household

What were Egyptian homes
made from?

c. Farmer, hunter,
craftsman

Egyptian men and women
both wore _____.

d. Mud bricks

Who were the PHARAOHS?

EGYPTIAN RULERS

The Pharaoh was the king in Ancient Egypt. He was the most important person in the land. The Egyptians believed that the Pharaohs were living Gods. Pharaohs had power but they also had many responsibilities. The Pharaoh was the commander in chief of the army, the religious leader, owned the land, made the laws, collected taxes, and performed many ceremonies throughout the year. The king had a special costume and headpiece to wear. He wore a diadem which was a headdress the shape of a cobra, ready to spit deadly defiance at his enemies. He wore a nemes, a striped cloth that hung on either side of the Pharaohs face. He also wore a false beard, a fake beard that was a symbol of his masculine strength. The Pharaoh couldn't marry just anyone, because he was considered a God! It was customary for a Pharaoh to marry someone from their own royal family. This was usually a close blood relative. They could have married a sister, half sister, or sometimes even their own daughters! A king spent some of his reign planning for his death by arranging and supervising the construction of his tomb. They believed in eternal life and that after death they would stay attached to their body and continue watching over the people in their land.

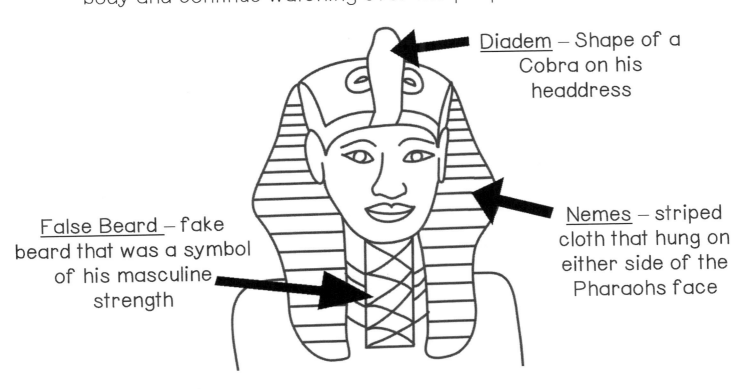

Diadem – Shape of a Cobra on his headdress

Nemes – striped cloth that hung on either side of the Pharaohs face

False Beard – fake beard that was a symbol of his masculine strength

EGYPTIAN RULERS

Read the passage. Use the passage to answer the questions. Use the correct color crayon to show where you found your answer in the text.

The Pharaoh was the king in Ancient Egypt. He was the most important person in the land. The Egyptians believed that the Pharaohs were living Gods. Pharaohs had power and many responsibilities. The Pharaoh was the commander in chief of the army, the religious leader, owned the land, made the laws, collected taxes, and performed many ceremonies. It was custom for a Pharaoh to marry someone from their own royal family. This was usually a close blood relative. When a Pharaoh died, he was buried in a special tomb.

1. What were two of the Pharaohs responsibilities?

_____

_____

2. Who could a Pharaoh marry?

_____

_____

EGYPTIAN RULERS

Label the parts of the pharaoh's headdress and attire. Color it the correct color.

False Beard – fake beard that was a symbol of his masculine strength

 Black

Diadem – Shape of a Cobra on his headdress, ready to spit deadly defiance at his enemies

 Yellow

Nemes – striped cloth that hung on either side of the Pharaohs face

 Blue

Pharaoh Khufu
Reigned from 2589 – 2566 BC

Khufu was a Fourth Dynasty pharaoh. He is most known for building the Great Pyramid of Giza, one of the Seven Wonders of the World. It was designed by Khufu as his stairway to heaven. The great pyramid is still standing today.

Pharaoh Hatshepsut
Reigned 1478–1458 BC

Hatshepsut was a Pharaoh who was also a woman. Hatshepsut was the wife of Thutmose II and reigned in the Eighteenth Dynasty. She was a good ruler, creating important trade routes and overseeing long periods of peace.

EGYPTIAN RULERS

Pharaoh Thutmose III
Reigned 1458–1425 BC

Thutmose III took over as pharaoh in 1458.
He had a reputation as a military genius.
Thutmose III never lost a battle, and this won
him the respect of his subjects. Many people
think of him as the greatest pharaoh ever.

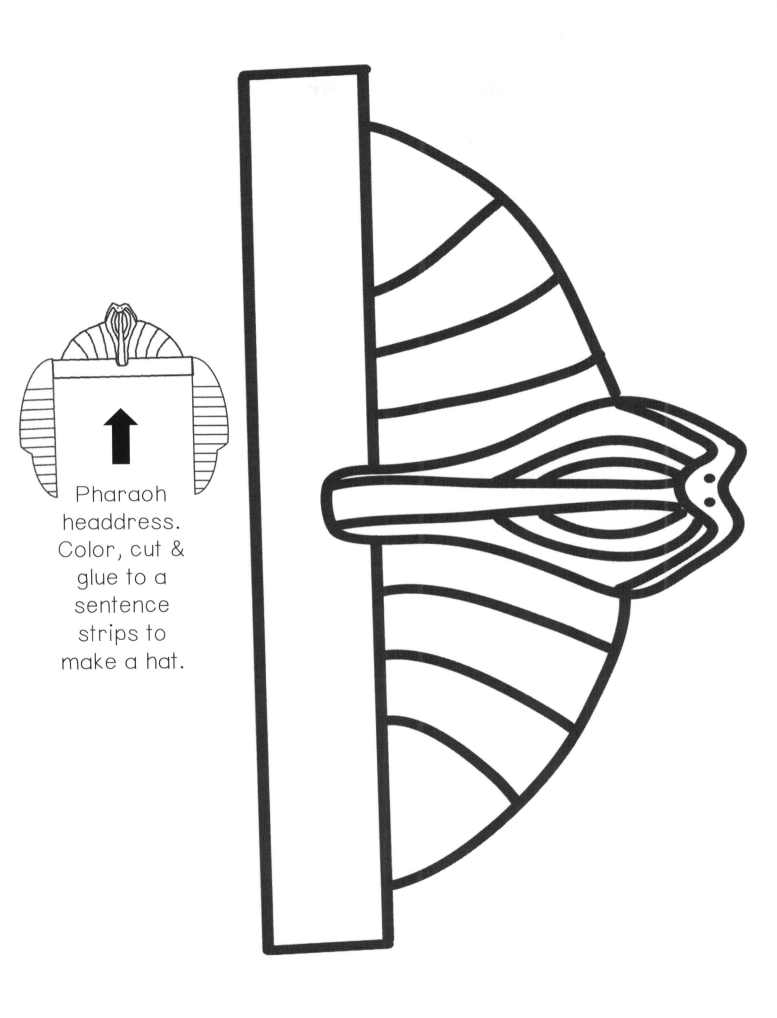

Pharaoh
headdress.
Color, cut &
glue to a
sentence
strips to
make a hat.

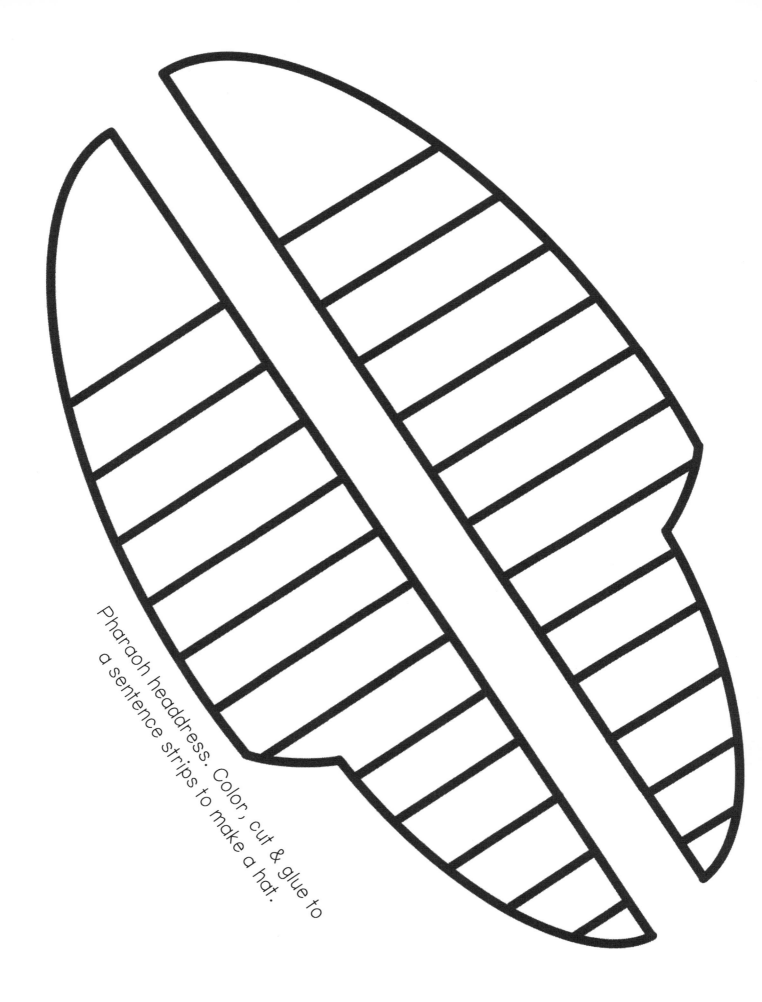

Pharaoh headdress. Color, cut & glue to
a sentence strips to make a hat.

EGYPTIAN RULERS

Search and find the words hidden in the word search!

E	G	Y	B	E	A	R	D	O	P
T	K	A	L	W	S	U	L	E	H
D	O	I	H	A	D	L	I	R	A
I	K	T	N	R	R	E	L	U	R
A	I	G	E	G	O	G	A	L	A
D	N	N	M	H	Y	H	W	E	O
E	H	I	E	I	A	J	S	T	H
M	D	L	S	E	L	L	S	Y	U
E	R	L	A	M	G	O	D	S	F
D	I	A	D	E	L	K	G	O	P

Pharaoh   Nemes   God

Ruler   King   Laws

Diadem   Beard   Royal

EGYPTIAN RULERS

What are three things you learned about Pharaoh's in ancient Egypt? Use complete sentences. Draw a picture to match in the box.

EGYPTIAN RULERS

After completing the "Egyptian Rulers" activities, take this quiz by **drawing a line** to the correct answer.

1. The Pharaoh was the _____ in Ancient Egypt.

   a. Religious leader, made the laws, collected taxes

2. What were some of the responsibilities of the Pharaoh?

   b. A close blood relative

3. Who could a Pharaoh marry?

   c. Diadem

4. Pharaohs wore special headdress with a _____ shaped like a cobra.

   d. King

Why did they build the PYRAMIDS?

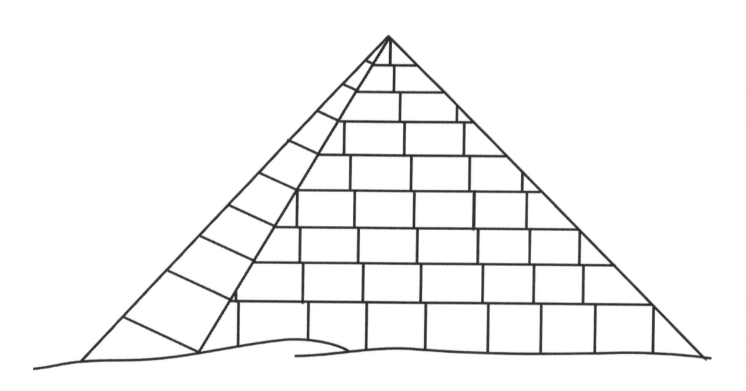

ANCIENT PYRAMIDS

In Ancient Egypt over 3,000 years ago, burial tombs for Pharaohs or kings were built for when they died. Some kings' tombs were built within stone or the ground. Others were built within HUGE pyramids. A pyramid had several rooms and long tunnels inside. The Pharaohs coffin was found in the burial room. The burial room was in the middle of the pyramid. Pyramids also held treasure! The ancient Egyptians believed in an afterlife. They filled the tomb with things they thought the pharaoh would need in the next life. They stored food, furniture, jewelry and weapons. Some tombs were even found with honey that was over 3,000 years old! Building the pyramids was very hard work. It took thousands of people to move the blocks into place. Each block weighed more than a car! Egyptologists believe that the ancient Egyptians used ramps to build the pyramids. The great pyramid was built with over 2.3 million stones! The pyramids in Giza, Egypt were built 4,500 years ago. They are still standing today. These Pyramids had smooth sides when they were built. Today the outer layer has mostly worn away.

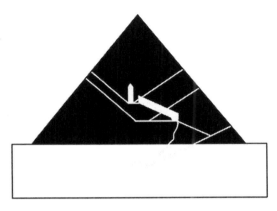

The tunnels and rooms inside a pyramid.

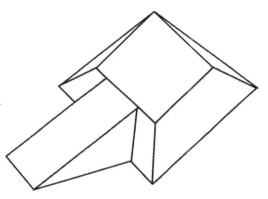

Drawing of a type of ramp the Egyptians might've used to build the pyramids!

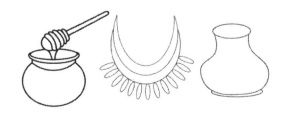

Treasure found inside the pyramids.

ANCIENT PYRAMIDS

Read the passage. Use the passage to answer the questions. Use the correct color crayon to show where you found your answer in the text.

The pyramids were tombs built for Pharaohs or kings for when they died. A pyramid had several rooms and long tunnels inside. The Pharaohs coffin was found in the burial room. The pyramids also held treasure! The ancient Egyptians believed in an afterlife so they filled the tomb with things the pharaoh would need in the next life. Some things they stored for the afterlife was food, furniture, jewelry and weapons. It took thousands of people to build the pyramids and move the blocks into place. Each block weighed more than a car! The pyramids took many years to build. Egyptologists believe that the ancient Egyptians used ramps to build the pyramids. Some pyramids are still standing today in Giza, Egypt!

1. What are two types of treasure found in pyramids?

_____

_____

2. How did Egyptians build the pyramids?

_____

_____

ANCIENT PYRAMIDS

Search and Find the words hidden in the ancient stones of the pyramid.

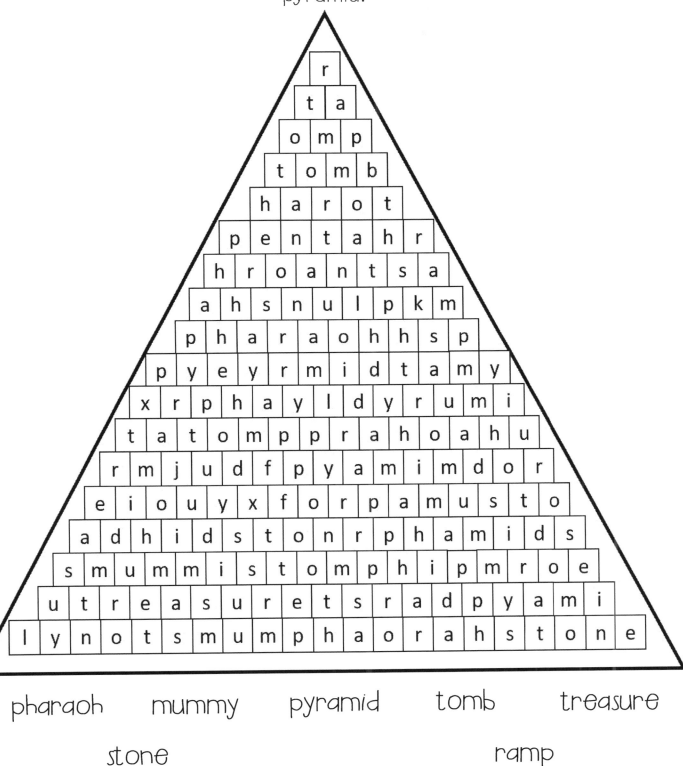

pharaoh   mummy   pyramid   tomb   treasure

stone   ramp

ANCIENT PYRAMIDS

Color the correct pyramid to answer the true or false question.

1. Pyramids were a temple that the Egyptians worshipped in.

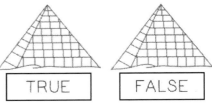

2. Only Pharaohs were buried in Pyramids.

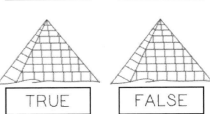

3. Pyramids held treasure, which were items for the Pharaoh to use in the afterlife.

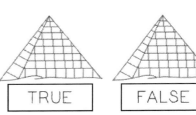

4. Pyramids were easy to build and only took a few years and a hundred men.

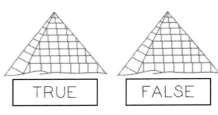

5. There are no pyramids left standing today.

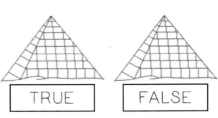

6. There are several rooms and long tunnels inside a pyramid.

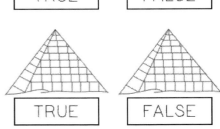

ANCIENT PYRAMIDS

Read the passage and color the pyramids below.

Pyramids Standing Today

These pyramids are the Great Pyramids of Giza. These pyramids are located near the Nile River, on the outskirts of modern-day Cairo. The oldest and largest of the three pyramids at Giza is known as the Great Pyramid. The Great Pyramid was built for Pharaoh Khufu. The middle pyramid at Giza was built for Khufu's son Pharaoh Khafre. The Pyramid of Khafre is the second tallest pyramid and contains Pharaoh Khafre's tomb. The smallest pyramid at Giza was built for Khafre's son Menkaure. You can visit these pyramids today, and even take a look inside!

ANCIENT PYRAMIDS

With the help of a grown up build a sugar cube pyramid. Sketch your design and fill out the sheet below.

MY PYRAMID DESIGN

SUGAR CUBES

Estimation: _____

Total Used: _____

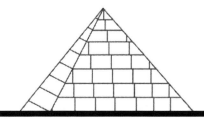

What was challenging about building your pyramid?

ANCIENT PYRAMIDS

Search and find the words hidden in the word search!

P	A	S	H	T	I	T	O	M	B
Y	S	B	O	A	L	R	I	C	F
R	E	L	A	M	P	E	K	O	K
A	A	O	R	V	L	A	N	F	I
M	S	C	A	X	A	S	I	F	N
I	F	K	H	O	S	U	F	I	C
D	G	S	P	M	A	R	F	N	H
I	H	L	E	I	E	E	B	I	A
T	U	N	N	S	M	U	M	M	Y
O	L	Y	A	T	U	N	N	E	L

Pyramid	Mummy	Treasure
Pharaoh	Blocks	Coffin
Tomb	Ramps	Tunnel

ANCIENT PYRAMIDS

If you designed a pyramid for the afterlife, what items would you store inside? Use complete sentences. Draw a picture to match in the box.

ANCIENT PYRAMIDS

After completing the "Ancient Pyramids" activities, take this quiz
by **drawing a line** to the correct answer.

1. Why were the pyramids built?

    a. Food, furniture, jewelry and weapons

2. How did the Egyptians build the pyramids?

    b. To be a tomb for Pharaohs when they died

3. What type of treasure would you find in a pyramid?

    c. Afterlife

4. Ancient Egyptians believed in an _____.

    d. With a ramp

What are MUMMIES?

MUMMIES

A mummy is a corpse that has been dried and embalmed so it will not decay. The Ancient Egyptians believed in an afterlife and that their bodies needed to be mummified when they died. The Egyptians believed that the mummified body was the home for the soul. If the body was destroyed, the soul might be lost. Special priests worked as embalmers to make mummies. They performed special rituals on the corpse and knew a lot about the human body. The chief embalmer would wear the mask of Anubis. Anubis was the jackal headed god of the dead. It took 70 days to make a mummy. First, embalmers pulled the organs like the brain, stomach and lungs out of the body and placed them in canopic jars. These jars would be stored near the mummy in the tomb. Next, The body needed to be dried out. It was rubbed with natron (a kind of salt) and left to dry for 40 days. Then, the body was cleaned, rubbed with oil, wax and gum to keep the skin from cracking. Then the corpse was stuffed with packing that was soaked in natron. After that, the body was wrapped in long strips of linen. Each layer was brushed in resin to make the linen bandages stick together. The wrapped body was given a portrait mask. This mask was made to look like the person inside. These masks were made of linen and plaster. Sometimes they were made of gold! Last, the mummy was laid in a coffin ready to be buried in their tomb. Sometimes the coffin would be placed in a decorative stone box called a sarcophagus.

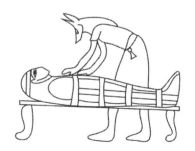  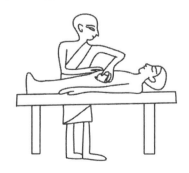

MUMMIES

Read the passage. Use the passage to answer the questions. Use the correct color crayon to show where you found your answer in the text.

A mummy is a corpse that has been dried and embalmed so it will not decay. The Egyptians believed in an afterlife and that their bodies needed to be mummified when they died. The Egyptians believed that the mummified body was the home for the soul. If the body was destroyed, the soul might be lost. Special priests worked as embalmers to make mummies. They performed rituals on the corpse and knew a lot about the human body. It took 70 days to make a mummy. First, embalmers pulled the organs out of the body and put them in canopic jars. Next, the body needed to be dried out! It was rubbed with natron (a kind of salt) and left to dry for 40 days. Then, the body was cleaned, rubbed with oil, wax and gum to keep the skin from cracking. Then the corpse was stuffed with packing that was soaked in natron. After that, the body was wrapped in long strips of linen. The wrapped body was given a portrait mask. Last, the mummy was laid in a coffin ready to be buried in their tomb.

1. . Why did the Egyptians make mummies?

_____

_____

2. How many days did it take to make a mummy?

_____

_____

MUMMIES

Read each step to learn how mummies are made. Color each step.

1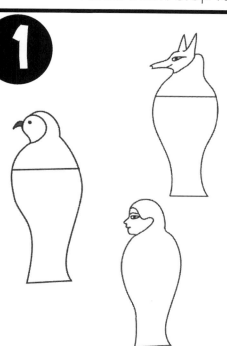

Organs placed in canopic jars

2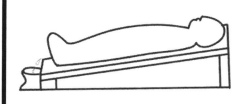

Body dries for 40 days

3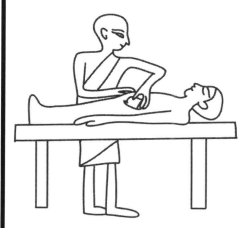

Body is rubbed in wax and oils and packed in Natron

4

Body wrapped in linen bandages

5

Wrapped body given a portrait mask

6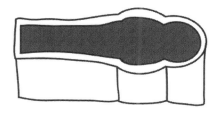

Mummy is placed in a coffin

MUMMIES

List and illustrate the steps the Ancient Egyptians took to make a mummy. Include as many details as you remember.

	_____

	_____

	_____

	_____

	_____

	_____

	_____

	_____

	_____

	_____

MUMMIES

Draw a line from each number to a box to put the steps of the mummification process in order.

 1

 2

 3

 4

 5

 6

Body dries for 40 days

Body wrapped in linen bandages

Mummy is placed in a coffin

Body is rubbed in wax and oils and packed in Natron

Organs placed in canopic jars

Wrapped body given a portrait mask

MUMMIES

Design this mummy a portrait mask. Be sure to give him or her a face, makeup and jewelry.

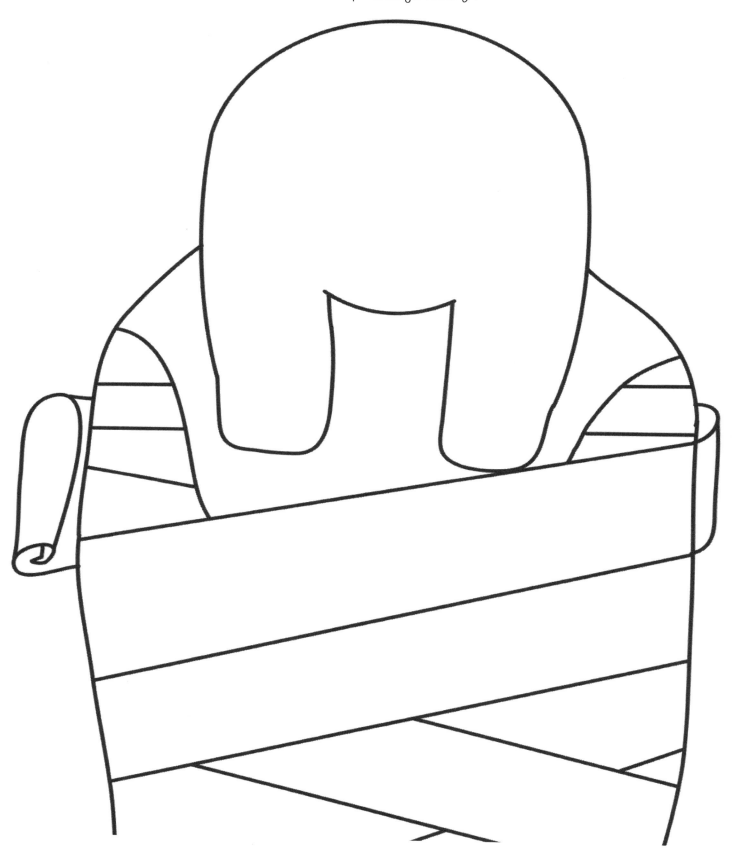

MUMMIES

Search and find the words hidden in the word search!

M	S	I	O	L	N	I	F	F	S
A	O	T	B	U	R	Y	C	C	D
K	U	R	U	Y	S	M	O	A	E
S	L	A	G	L	I	A	F	N	T
D	H	E	G	A	Y	S	F	O	P
I	L	I	N	E	N	K	I	P	M
A	T	O	M	B	K	S	N	I	B
F	N	O	P	I	S	O	U	C	L
N	A	T	R	O	N	F	I	N	E
G	O	R	G	A	S	N	D	L	T

Organs   Tomb   Soul

Canopic   Bury   Linen

Natron   Mask   Coffin

MUMMIES

How and why did the Egyptians make mummies? Use complete sentences.
Draw a picture to match in the box.

MUMMIES

After completing the "Mummies" activities, take this quiz by **drawing a line** to the correct answer.

1. How long did it take to make a mummy?

a. 40 days

2. What were the mummies organs stored in?

b. 70 Days

3. Who was in charge of making the mummies?

c. Special priests called embalmers

4. How long was the body left to dry before it was wrapped?

d. Canopic Jars

What are HIEROGLYPHICS?

HIEROGLYPHICS

In ancient Egypt, scribes were some of the only people who could read and write. They went to school for 10 to 12 years to learn to write in hieroglyphics! Hieroglyphics are symbols that represent a letter, sound or idea. There were over 800 different hieroglyphics! Many are pictures of animals, people or objects. Egyptians used hieroglyphics for 3,500 years. Then about 1,000 years ago they stopped using them. Their meaning was lost, and no one remembered how to read them. Then, in 1822, a French scholar named Jean-Francois Champollion figured out how to decode hieroglyphics! He used a stone tablet called the Rosetta Stone to crack the code. It had 3 types of writing on it, one was ancient Greek which he could read, and one was Egyptian hieroglyphics! Now we can read and write in hieroglyphics just like ancient Egyptian scribes! Nearly all Egyptian documents were written down by scribes on scrolls made of papyrus. Scribes used tools that were a lot like watercolors. Scribes kept their colors and tools in a wooden box. Inside the box was a palette of colors and pens made of reeds. They had to dip the pen in water to use the colors. In hieroglyphic writing, the name of a ruler was surrounded by an oval. This was called a cartouche. Egyptians made cartouches to wear as amulets, and charms for good luck!

Scribe

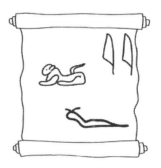

Papyrus Scroll

Egytpian
Writing Tools

Cartouche

HIEROGLYPHICS

Read the passage. Use the passage to answer the questions. Use the correct color crayon to show where you found your answer in the text.

In ancient Egypt, scribes were some of the only people who could read and write. They went to school for 10 to 12 years to learn to write in hieroglyphics! Hieroglyphics are symbols that represent a letter, sound or idea. Many are pictures of animals, people or objects. Nearly all Egyptian documents were written down by scribes on scrolls made of papyrus. To write their scrolls, scribes used tools that were a lot like watercolors. Scribes kept their colors and tools in a wooden box. Inside the box was a palette of colors and pens made of reeds. In hieroglyphic writing, the name of a ruler was surrounded by an oval. This was called a cartouche. Egyptians made cartouches to wear as amulets and as charms for good luck!

1. . How long did scribes go to school?

_____

_____

2. What were scrolls made of?

_____

_____

a	b	c	d	e	f	g	h	i	j	k	l	m
n	o	p	q	r	s	t	u	v	w	x	y	z

Directions: Use the Hieroglyphic code above to figure out the words in the boxes.

HIEROGLYPHICS	WORD

HIEROGLYPHICS

Pretend you are an ancient Egyptian scribe. Use the chart below to write the words in hieroglyphics.

a	b	c	d	e	f	g	h	i	j	k	l	m

n	o	p	q	r	s	t	u	v	w	x	y	z

HIEROGLYPHICS	WORD
	Pharaoh
	Scribe
	Egypt
	Nile
	Mummy
	Pyramid
	Cartouche

HIEROGLYPHICS

Use the chart to sketch your name in the cartouche.

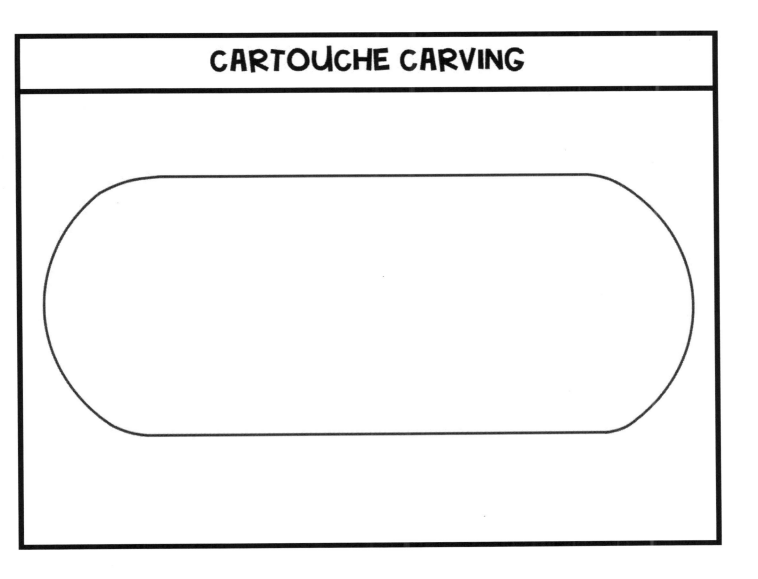

CARTOUCHE CARVING

HIEROGLYPHICS

Pretend you are an ancient Egyptian scribe. Use the chart below to create your own hieroglyphic symbol for each alphabet letter. Use these symbols to write words using your hieroglyphic chart.

a	b	c	d	e	f	g	h	i	j	k	l	m

n	o	p	q	r	s	t	u	v	w	x	y	z

HIEROGLYPHICS	WORD

HIEROGLYPHICS

Search and find the words hidden in the word search!

P	A	P	Y	T	U	S	S	C	R
A	S	T	U	D	E	N	T	R	W
P	C	R	E	E	S	D	T	E	R
Y	R	A	S	C	H	O	O	L	I
R	S	I	C	E	T	S	H	Y	T
U	C	A	R	T	O	U	C	H	E
S	R	N	I	B	M	C	X	E	N
N	O	T	B	C	H	A	R	M	S
E	L	R	E	Y	R	E	E	D	S
S	L	C	R	O	K	L	C	H	A

Cartouche   Student   Charms

Scribe   Write   Scroll

School   Reeds   Papyrus

HIEROGLYPHICS

How did an Egyptian become a scribe? What tools would they use? Use complete sentences. Draw a picture to match in the box.

HIEROGLYPHICS

After completing the "Hieroglyphics" activities, take this quiz by **drawing a line** to the correct answer.

1. In ancient Egypt, who knew how to write in hieroglyphics?

   a. Over 800

2. How many different types of hieroglyphics are there?

   b. Scrolls of papyrus

3. What did Egyptian scribes write on?

   c. Reeds

4. What was a scribe's pen made of?

   d. Scribes

What is Egypt like TODAY?

MODERN DAY EGYPT

Egypt today is very different than it was in ancient times. Egypt is no longer ruled by a pharaoh. Egypt now has a democracy. Instead of having a king as their ruler, the people vote for a president who serves for six years. In Cairo you can still travel to see the pyramids. Cairo and most of Egypt's big cities also have skyscrapers, paved roads, hotels, restaurants, western clothing, and ancient monuments all mixed together. If you visit Egypt and want to see ancient artifacts, be sure to visit a museum to see the ancient statues, royal mummies, papyrus scrolls, intricate jewelry, and even children's toys from long ago!

MODERN DAY EGYPT

Read the passage. Use the passage to answer the questions. Use the correct color crayon to show where you found your answer in the text.

Egypt today is very different than it was in ancient times. Egypt is no longer ruled by a pharaoh. Egypt now has a democracy. Instead of having a king as their ruler, the people vote for a president who serves for six years. In Cairo you can still travel to see the pyramids. Cairo and most of Egypt's big cities also have skyscrapers, paved roads, hotels, restaurants, western clothing, and ancient monuments all mixed together. If you visit Egypt be sure to visit a museum to see huge statues, royal mummies, papyrus scrolls, intricate jewelry, and even children's toys from long ago!

1. How many years does the president serve?

_____

_____

2. What are two things you might see if you visit Egypt today?

_____

_____

MODERN DAY EGYPT

Color the correct pyramid to answer the true or false question.

1. Modern Egypt is run by Pharaohs.

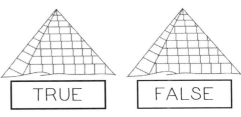

TRUE   FALSE

2. Egypt is very different now than it was in ancient times.

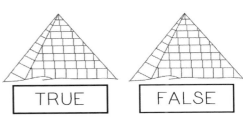

TRUE   FALSE

3. Egypt no longer exists.

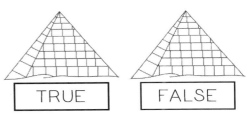

TRUE   FALSE

4. Egypt now has a democracy.

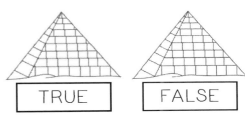

TRUE   FALSE

5. There are no pyramids left standing today.

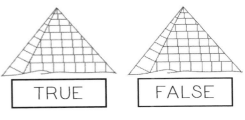

TRUE   FALSE

6. You can see an Egyptian mummy in a museum.

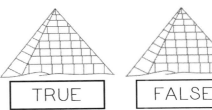

TRUE   FALSE

MODERN DAY EGYPT

Search and find the words hidden in the word search!

P	R	E	S	I	D	E	N	T	Z
E	G	P	A	S	E	P	I	R	Y
A	H	Y	N	C	M	L	C	A	T
R	O	T	C	V	O	T	E	V	I
C	T	A	I	Y	C	O	D	E	C
O	E	N	E	D	R	H	E	L	S
M	L	C	N	E	A	V	R	A	D
E	T	I	T	R	C	E	O	A	D
D	I	T	A	N	Y	I	N	P	F
E	M	O	D	E	R	N	T	O	I

President   City   Modern

Democracy   Road   Ancient

Vote   Hotel   Travel

MODERN DAY EGYPT

If you visited Egypt today, what would you see? Use complete sentences.
Draw a picture to match in the box.

MODERN DAY EGYPT

After completing the "Modern Day Egypt" activities, take this quiz
by **drawing a line** to the correct answer.

1. In ancient Egypt, who ran
    the government?

                                                    a. Cities

2. In modern Egypt who ran
    the government?

                                                    b. Pharaoh

3. Cairo and most of Egypt's
    big _____ have paved
    roads, skyscrapers and
    more.   c. Museum

4. If you want to see an   d. President
    ancient Egyptian artifact,
    where can you go?

Printed in Great Britain
by Amazon